NEFARIOUS

"Brash, dark, funny-Emanuel Xavier is all these things, but more important, he is ruthlessly true, brutally kind, painfully relevant and terribly gifted." —**Trebor Healey**, author of *A Horse Named Sorrow*

"These poems are eloquent snapshots from a real life, full of emotion, fact, and surprise. Emanuel Xavier can take you from the brutal to the tender to the sexual to the religious in the blink of an eye--or from the prosy to the lyrical to the laugh-out-loud funny. His poems put you in touch with the whole man, his bone and gristle, heart and soul." —**Christopher Bram**, author of *Eminent Outlaws: The Gay Writers Who Changed America*

Jim—
Much love always!
Emanuel
Xavier

NEFARIOUS

Emanuel Xavier

QUEER MOJO
A Rebel Satori Imprint
Bar Harbor, Maine

Cover Photo: Emanuel Xavier
Author Photo: Sophia Wallace
Book Design: Sven Davisson

ISBN: 978-1-60864-094-2

Rebel Satori Press
P.O. Box 363
Hulls Cove, ME 04644

Library of Congress Cataloging-in-Publication Data

Xavier, Emanuel.
  [Poems. Selections]
  Nefarious : poems / by Emanuel Xavier.
    pages cm
  ISBN 978-1-60864-094-2 (pbk.)
  I. Title.
  PS3574.A85A6 2013
  811'.54--dc23

                    2013034356

Grateful acknowledgment is made to the following publications in which these poems first originally appeared:

"Mi Corazón", "Conquest" and "Missing" appeared in *Me No Habla With Acento: Contemporary Latino Poetry*, El Museo del Barrio/ Rebel Satori Press, 2011

"Revelation" appeared in *Assaracus: A Journal of Gay Poetry*, Issue 4

"Los Hijos de Magdalena" appeared in English in *Americano: Growing Up Gay and Latino in the USA*, Rebel Satori Press, 2012

"Naked" appeared in *Kin Poetry Journal*, 2013

"Golden Shower at a Motel 6 in San Antonio", "Step Father", "Savior" and "The Way We Are (or Perhaps Just the Way That I Am)" appeared in *Assaracus: A Journal of Gay Poetry*, Issue 12

"Step Father" appeared in *Poetry Nook Magazine*, 2013

CONTENTS

RUNAWAY	1
SCREEN TEST	2
EL HAIR ESPRAY	3
THE ESCAPE ARTIST	5
ENCOUNTER	6
REVELATION	8
PREY	10
THE THING ABOUT MY PUSSY	12
GOLDEN SHOWER AT A MOTEL 6 IN SAN ANTONIO	14
GL' AMOUR	17
ASCENDING THE MOUNTAIN	18
MI CORAZÓN	20
CONQUEST	22
MISSING	24
GAY MAN ATTACKED IN BUSHWICK	25
ROUGH	26
EUCHARIST OF THE REFORMED WHORE	27
MEMORABLE	52
REDUNDANT	53
DEAD	55
HATS OFF TO THE BULL	58
TRESPASS	59
LOS HIJOS DE MAGDALENA	60
THE REASON	61
MARRIAGE & BONUS REWARD POINTS	62
FORSAKEN	64
THE HUSTLER	67
NAKED	69
SAVIOR	70
UNBLOSSOMED	73
WHY IT TOOK SO LONG	76
STEP FATHER	79

Boy Running on Palmetto Street, Bushwick, June 1985
(original image full color) © Meryl Meisler 1985

RUNAWAY

For Meryl Meisler

There is a world out there where I belong:
loved by a mother and father who understand
my dreams, who listen to my fears of my older

cousin, his touch, or how boys make fun of me
in school. There is a world out there where I can
grow up to love myself and others like me, where

soft spoken boys can speak boldly. I will
call it, poetry, each memory an inspiration. All
this pain, these dismembered and abandoned cars,

these empty lots left behind where I know deep
in my heart that there is innocence in playing
with dolls, reaching for rainbows, books, even *mami's*

pretty dresses. I will not be alone in this world.
I have somewhere to run. I do not know exactly
where. I have no maps or stars to guide me through

the night. If it turns out that this is my world,
maybe I should simply learn to laugh and live
and let the others catch up to me instead.

SCREEN TEST

Try to convince him you are innocent, you no longer crave
     darkness. He will think he loves you. Treat him
affectionately. Get him to pick you up in his car,

take you away for a weekend. His friends and family
     adore you. Pretend you trusted him while he was in
Australia. Express pain over that text message

he got from a couple looking for a third while he was
     showering. Watch as he avoids eye contact and know this
(whatever this is) is over. Continue having raw sex with him

to settle any doubts and trust your devotion. Book a major
     gig and plan a trip to California. You will be a star.
On stage, in front of your audience, perhaps he will finally feel

something. This will add more scars to his face, already filled
     with journeys through denial. You will know this is killing
him—the closeted Republican fucking the openly gay artist.

You hate his self-hatred, that his friends think he is sweet.
     Wait until he breaks up with you (a week before Christmas).
Tell him you will delete him as a friend on Facebook. Refuse to

let him drive you home. Let him think he hurt you badly, and
     you didn't see it coming. Force yourself to cry. Never let him
see you smile. He will think he is finally free. Get tested.

EL HAIR ESPRAY

When it came to music, the only thing she ever really knew about me was that I was turned on to Madonna after seeing her in concert. At least *abuela* indulged my tendencies by introducing me to Sarita Montiel but *mami* was in love with Venezuelan singer Jose Luis Rodriguez. She had half-naked posters of him plastered on her bedroom wall that I often fantasized about. He wasn't my type but I wouldn't have thrown him out of bed though *mami* always said, *"There's a special place in hell for child molesters AND the sexy little boys that seduce them."* This was before she found out about her cousin and me in the Coney Island projects when I was much younger.

It was odd that a woman in her thirties with a son that was obviously gay would hang homoerotic imagery in the household. Let alone the room she shared with my stepfather who was taunted and cuckolded by the singer Puerto Rican fans nicknamed "El Puma." I suppose my posters of Boy George perhaps made him question exactly what kind of family he had taken residence with. We both wondered if El Puma was, in fact, my real father.

When I let my hair grow out in the 80s, much like her idol, my mother was convinced I was paying tribute to his long feathered locks. Never mind the fact that real pumas don't even have a mane. It was when I bleached it orange-red that she realized my inspiration was actually Cyndi Lauper. She was furious at my oblivious feminine ways but somehow convinced herself I was destined to become her mini Puma. Though, in the end, I looked more like a tween Walter Mercado.

El Puma starred in several *telenovelas* she watched religiously as I learned my lines from "Dynasty." She never understood why I had no appreciation for Spanish music or television. Her favorite

3

song was El Puma's "Pavo Real," a song about … wait for it…
peacocks. The irony of a man named after a large cat singing about
flamboyant male birds never dawned on her. I suppose he should
have been right up my alley with his hairy chest and dark features
but quite frankly my jitterbug belonged to George Michael. When
it came to music, we were *agua y fuego*. Not even freestyle music
and Lisa Lisa's mullet could bring us together.

It wasn't until Gloria Estefan burst onto the music scene with the
same hairdo as El Puma that mother, son, and *gringo's* all over the
country fell in love with "The Conga." The Miami Sound Machine
bridged all of our differences and brought everyone to the party
and under the *escoba*. We were foreign, even to each other, but
this one crossover hit made us a true 80s American *familia*—full
of beauty, perhaps a little bit broken, but with really big hair. As
for El Puma, my mother never lost her *cabeza por su amor* and it
turned out he wasn't my father after all.

THE ESCAPE ARTIST

My cat's entire universe is our apartment much like my *abuelas* consists of only Bushwick. This reality reminds me of my childhood sleeping on a sofa bed in a small living room. For years, it was my sanctuary as my mother and stepfather had loud sex and fights in the bedroom. They only left the apartment to go shopping. I would stay behind and play with my superhero action figures, pretending they were real and would save me as I donned a towel for long, luscious hair and was kidnapped by villains. The furniture were mountains and only my 12–inch Superman doll or Six Million Dollar Man could rescue me. The only window to the outside world faced another building with an alley for the dumpsters between them. It was only when Johnny—the toned, often shirtless, Puerto Rican teen from the other building—threw out the garbage that I would gaze from behind the curtains fantasizing that he would be the one to set me free. "Why you staring at my brother like that?" his hateful little sister once yelled as I dropped the toilet roll center that had become my makeshift binocular. I remember watching "The Shining" that night and wondering where in this giant empty hotel of our living room I would hide if my stepfather found out and tried to kill me. There was no place for me to run but when I closed my eyes to sleep I could fly. I could be a beautiful blonde haired, blue eyed, big tittied teenage girl in Daisy Dukes cut off jean shorts throwing out the trash for that bitch's brother to fall in love and ride away with on his motorcycle. Yeah, that's how fucked up and twisted life was for a self-hating gay little Latin boy without friends or his own bedroom as a child. All there was to look forward to was being left behind to play with my own imagination, late night television and sleep. I volunteered to start throwing out the garbage from that day on.

ENCOUNTER

I have been looking for you
since the moment I accepted as a
teen that I was attracted to other
men and learned to love myself,
even after my mother gave up on
me the way my father had discarded
us, since I sold myself on the streets
hoping to find you in all the men
I let take advantage of my misfortune
as long as they paid for my love.

I have been looking for you
since I found my way back home,
overcame the past and started writing
poems to reclaim my soul, since I
kept falling in love with all the men
that weren't you, thinking perhaps you
did not exist, even as I stared out at the
stars and knew you too might find them
in the night sky and someday look into
my eyes to watch them shine for you.

I have been looking for you
since confessing all of my
weaknesses in front of audiences
hoping to find you amongst them,
since exposing my life with abandon
so that you would never leave me once
we met, since I whored myself in
denial that you were still out there
somewhere, since settling for anyone
who could just make me smile.

6

I have been looking for you
since staring out the window
watching storms pass by, listening
to winds pick up, since I found
myself getting older with my cat, since
my best friend enjoyed the same sex
marriage I had hoped for us as well,
since I realized I had no religion to pray
for you to come into this world, since I
convinced myself that I was happy.

I have been looking for you
since this neighborhood changed
from a ghetto where I almost died
to an artist sanctuary where I thrive,
since I look in the mirror and find it
difficult to find that petty angry
criminal that once lived inside me,
since the love songs I grew up singing
to you became retro classics, since my
small book collection became a library.

I have been looking for you
since I lost all of the hearing in one
ear, it became harder to stay in shape,
my diet no longer included carbs and
sugars, since I needed more sleep to get
through the days, since the moment
I realized I spent all of this life searching
and that I might never find you, since we
kissed and I became hopeful
once again that I had finally found you.

REVELATION

for Rane Arroyo

It was the chocolate brown walls he had painted
in anticipation of his lovers move from another state,
The soft cuddle of his cat laying on his chest as he read poetry
the way he had imagined his lover would
It was the way the leaves had turned from green to yellow to red
and the brutal winter had covered the ground with a multitude of
white snow without ever hearing the sound of his voice
He reminisced about how they met and what they had promised
to each other, the trips back and forth and the plans that had
been set with bodies intertwined
looking through the branches up at the limitless sky

Now he lived alone with his pet surrounded
by the colors of this purgatory and
vases without arrangements, leaks that required fixing,
furniture lacking his scent
It had surprisingly shifted his entire balance—
another man who had simply vanished,
evaporated into the now thick air with nothing left behind
but lonely reflections in the mirror
It was death all over again, this room designed to be his coffin,
waiting for life to pass as everyone else
found love with ease and left him behind

He contemplated dating again as soon as
the bitter wind changed direction
from the city where he became a man
and each street reminded him of loss
It would be in deep brown or blue or green eyes
 that he would forget the failure of fathers,

that books had been his brothers, songs had been his sisters
His touch would prove this existence
That someone was capable of loving him,
even if his background was a wild river most feared crossing

He looked to find his residence in the words of others
but found nothing
Until he came across the line,
"I stop dreaming so I can return home"
Now he could believe once again without naiveté that poetry
always demands all of our ghosts
Perhaps, even at this age, doubt would not delude his desire
With just one haunting sentence he was brought back to life

PREY

i.

Two cousins sharing a bed in South America—
the eleven-year-old one, from New York,
teaching a fifteen-year-old how to masturbate.

Surprised the older teen freaked out when he came
and claimed he had seen angels at the edge of the bed
watching over them.

Feeling guilty that he had perpetuated a sinful act
when he thought he was doing a late bloomer a major favor.

After all, it was a fifteen-year-old cousin that had taught him
about sex when he was three.

ii.

The first time was not really the first time
Maybe this is why he remembered little of it.

The guy had been a struggling actor, much older,
with an apartment somewhere in Queens.

That made him rich and worthy of disenfranchised illegal desire.
A copy of *The Joy of Gay Sex* and a bottle of champagne
was all it took.

He led the underage boy who had lied about his age onto his bed
and popped in some VHS porn flick. Later, he dropped him
off at a subway station wondering if he was really a virgin.

iii.

His lover lay in bed holding him—
their silly-looking slippers off to the side.

They could have met years ago and shared many stories
but both had hoped that night a decade ago
that the other would be the first one to make a move.

Now they watch rented movies on the DVD, laugh about their
misfortunes and cuddle under the thick winter quilts
before falling asleep together.

No ghosts or angels or Christ haunting them,
only loud prostitutes on the Brooklyn street corner

outside—cold, weathered, waiting for the next trick.

THE THING ABOUT MY PUSSY

My pussy has lots of dreams for us. There is no room for anyone else in our universe.

We are atheists but believe there will be an afterlife for us to continue this wondrous journey. My pussy is very political.

When the time comes, my pussy has requested to be cremated as the thought of long, slimy worms crawling inside sounds gross.

My pussy chews on my pens as I try to write. My pussy does not realize he is acting in a way inappropriate to his age. My pussy refuses to grow up. Perhaps my pussy thinks it is Halloween. But then he is black and everyday is a Satanic holiday to him.

My pussy has money stored away somewhere in this apartment and a collection of thongs he wears in the summer when I am not home.

I don't know where that rumor about pussies stealing your breath at night came from. My pussy's only goal is to get me to fall asleep so that we could cuddle.

I have yet to find that hidden camera I know my pussy had installed to film me while having sex with men. One day my pussy will blackmail me for some expensive Japanese dinner or these will end up on the internet.

My pussy is not satisfied that I gave him a drag queen name and had his balls removed at an early age so that he wouldn't have to tuck.

My pussy has saved me on numerous occasions from villains that have broken into our home and attempted to murder me. He does not care that New York is not a stand your ground state.

My pussy maintains his glorious physique by purposefully swallowing his own hair and does not understand his warped influence on young impressionable girls insecure about their weight.

My pussy is a great host and welcomes all of our guests with such flair. He loves corduroy and contemporary pop music.

My pussy is a huge fan of graffiti art and period piece movies. My pussy likes poetry and humorous short story collections but has been known to read chick lit during the summer season. I wouldn't put it past him to tag the neighborhood walls dressed as a character from a Jane Austen novel.

My pussy is rather superstitious and hates the Pope, Republicans, onions, Jehovah's Witnesses, Chris Brown and anyone allergic to pussy.

GOLDEN SHOWER AT A MOTEL 6 IN SAN ANTONIO

It is quite unexpected.
He is extremely drunk.
Sexy body. Pretty boy
Mexican. He comes back
to my room at the Motel 6,
French kissing in the cab.
I'm surprised he doesn't mama bird
me in the back seat. It is too late
to send him home.
We undress.
I figured we could cuddle
all night long in each other's arms
before morning sex.
Comfort from a recent break up.
We mess around naked.
Fall asleep like long time lovers.
In the middle of the night,
I smell a foul stench in the air.
With the bathroom only
a few feet away,
his urine soaks
into the sheets, wetness
creeps toward my legs, he giggles.
I have willingly enjoyed
a playful piss from a lover
in the shower as an act of love.
Perhaps I've participated
in water sports with kinky men.
But I have never had anyone
pull a #1 while laying
next to me in some cheap motel.
He continues to sleep.
I stare at the ceiling horrified.

If he was embarrassed,
he simply casually moves
the stained bedsheets to the side,
embraces me.
In his twenties, he was too old
for diapers. Too young for medical
issues. Waking him up seemed
foolish. Yes, I don't want to
shame him or shove his face
into the yellowed fabric
to train him like my cat.
I wondered if he still expects
me to suck him off
when the sun comes up.
Tomorrow, I'll call him Pee Diddy!
I'm afraid to think what 'getting
shit-faced' might mean in his universe.
Will he tell his friends?
I am now sleepless
with the thought of having been dumped
and then literally pissed on.
I would be the one to pick up
the guy with bladder problems
who can't control his flow.
This was supposed to be
about connecting with another man—
one who wore big boy pants.
It's a good thing I've slept through
several interesting situations.
I drift off—eventually
awakening to find him staring
down at me. He is hungry
and goes down. My cock
responds dutifully as my eyes
search for the crumpled, tossed
victim. I want to grab my cell

and phone-a-friend but he might
notice. For all of his hard work,
I can't cum. We chit chat instead,
he gets quickly dressed, I call him
a cab. We never mention it—the
smelly Big Bird in the room.
We kiss and hug to seal the moment.
It's a bittersweet goodbye, perhaps
more bitter than sweet—the kind soldiers
give each other while dead bodies
rot just a few feet away.
What will the cleaning lady think?
I guess I'll have to tip her well.
I worry she'll think it was me—
an adult guest staying at a Motel 6,
near a pool, fresh, clean toilet,
dirty laundry—soaked with minerals—
a little boy scared of the dark.

GL' AMOUR

I post a shirtless selfie hugging my cat on my public Facebook page
hoping the guy I just made out with on Friday night
will take notice.
I am happy to finally get a 'Like' out of him.
Fans comment but only his response counts.
I will not see him again for weeks until he returns from Europe
or maybe never again. He will not know that I am fragile.
As per articles he will google on the internet,
I know how to survive. Anyone
can read how I was abandoned—left behind to fade,
not featured on milk cartons, supposed to be forgotten,
just quietly disappear.
Perhaps all I need is Christ, perhaps an
animal. As I wait to someday taste his lips again, I just sleep
a lot and take naps with my pet. We cuddle
and he sleeps in my arms, as if he were him, knowing
he can't return the favor
while his little claws rest within furry paws.
He twitches from a nightmare. I wonder can he sense
the loneliness I feel—the single life challenge
even I cannot overcome. I have made it this far but,
indeed, all by myself. I hold him
tight—the father or lover I never met
and hope this new obsession might be,
or the God supposed to watch over me from the balcony of heaven,
a peephole in the open sky, footsteps in sand
carrying me at the beach
or shoe imprints in glitter as he lifts me out of the nightclub
and the credits roll.
I am thinking this is it for me,
while he is somewhere on his plane up in the clouds
without a need to be held.

ASCENDING THE MOUNTAIN

I cannot levitate two feet off the ground and bring
      back children from the dead

I am not amongst the two and a half hundred thousand of the
      greatest, most virtuous human beings that ever lived or a
miniaturized three—dimensional version of them

My spoken word will not entertain appreciative fish and
      guarantee my lower jaw to be enshrined after my death

I do not believe Adam lived to be 930 or that Noah lived to be
      950 or that Enoch is immortal because of your grace and
would now be over 5,000 years old

I don't offer you thanks every time I eat a new fruit, or acquire a
      new garment of significant value or digest my food

If I were to eventually go bald and be made fun of by 42
      children, unlike Elijah, I will not curse them in your name
and have them mauled to death by two female bears

When in love, I will not kill over 100 men and make offerings
      of their foreskins no matter how hot the bitch (or stud)

I will not curse a fig tree to death because it is off-season and
      this inanimate object does not respond to my abuse of power
because I am hungry

I do not make the sign of the cross everytime I pass one of
      those buildings with the small letter t on top of them

I suppose I have failed you much like you did as a father

Be that as it may, let's call it even
Still I think I know more about you than most of your followers

Perhaps I will never see your face and, like Moses, you will show
me your backside instead and I will think you're so gay

MI CORAZÓN

I search for my soul in paintbrush strokes
listen for my muse in Mr. Softee ice cream truck jingles
smile at strangers on the subway for simple humanity
This heart seems a novelty but it continues to love

It makes children out of full-grown men
withdraws the instinctive awareness of animals
It beats enough passion to arouse poetry
etching words that mean nothing yet everything

Like drums and like songs
with the conviction of dance
Like rhythm flowing from bodies
It continues to love

It has outlived history like a vampire
blood healed and stronger with time
Beauty resounding from within
Bathed in tears and sheltered from the bruises outside

City noises drown the thumping sounds
Threatened to be frozen by bitter cold
but it beats to the tune of glimmering eyes
as it unfolds to render a lonesome petal

Concrete may not supply cushion
Perverse lights may weaken the stars it craves
Hatred may wage war and hindrance
but it continues to love

It reveals itself through a kiss
The same which often hides it

Often remembered and rather forgotten
like skyscrapers offering great views but obstructing the sky

An abandoned pier surrounded by polluted rivers
It continues to love
Walls torn down for a better view of the other side
It continues to love

Projects housing poverty and lifeless dreams
elevators hauling empty designer pockets
gateways to famine and drought
It continues to love

Into nights brightened by moon
It continues to love

Life as offered by family and friends
It is the salvation and prayer for forgiveness
It continues to love

It continues
to love

CONQUEST

Your absence is the pillow used to cuddle at night, with you next to
me, as the moon watches over the despair of this darkness.

Distant and cold like the snow of mountains.
It is my cue to leave in the morning.

This rose, my heart, will not have sunlight to bloom here.
Tears will not provide enough rain to sustain this life.

Your demons revel in their fire.
Your songs lure another shipwrecked soul.

Your beauty disguises your myths, like religion.
Wars waged without necessity, out of fear.

What brought us to the tomb of this bed was only meant to be a
dramatic kiss, hope between wounded soldiers on a stage.

I should have tasted the blood on your lips,
caught a glimpse of a deadbeat father in your eyes.

You shot with fair warning, celebrated your victory,
heroic in your justice of killing the child with stolen toy in hand.

I will not be meaningful enough to haunt you
beyond words and I will be forgotten.

It was not your duty to hold me in your arms
without holding back and, for this, I grant you atonement.

Like the morning sun, dreams were awakened by your light
and quickly faded as reality set back in.

There was loneliness and sadness, and you were the hope.
There was violence and pain, and you were the healing.

Others will undoubtedly drown in the sea of your emotions,
get lost in your conflicts; continue to be music for the masses.

Our time shared crossing this path was insignificant—when you get
to greener pastures, enjoy the air, breeze against your skin.

I will perhaps be a story maybe worth sharing, nothing more.

MISSING

I apologize to you now
for holding back what you should know
but there are too many expectations of me
that are my own fault for sharing my life in such detail.
I have never been good at keeping things to myself
publicly sharing what most would deem personal
but I'm learning to build walls again.

Those that actually read my words look between the lines,
"Is this what he is really like?" Perhaps.
One day, you will find me again at the amusement park
I will be the little boy with the red balloon,
a runaway who found himself,
a life fulfilled prepared for death.

It was never your responsibility to save me
Others didn't recognize me from milk cartons either.
You might think I am giving you the stink eye
When, in fact, I will no longer be just half deaf but fully blind.
I will be gone as soon as you look away.

When you spot the balloon in the sky
You will realize that it wasn't a dream.
The brightness of the sun will not wash away the red.
Someday you'll see me yet again, when the time is right,
Make sure to point me out to your friends
at the amusement park, the little half deaf blind boy
with the red balloon in front of the graffitied wall.

GAY MAN ATTACKED IN BUSHWICK

On the evening of Tuesday, October 25, 2005, a gay man is brutally attacked in Bushwick, NY by a group of teenagers.

He obviously made some sexual innuendo at one of those innocent young boys as they all walked past him, staring at their teenage bulges. Dangerous predators like him are always up to no good, they can't keep their hands to themselves, perverting everything.

Perhaps he had inappropriately touched one of their little brothers who was underage and they had been looking for him throughout the neighborhood. The boy was traumatized and had tried to kill himself, he didn't want to turn out gay or grow up to be a pervert too. For days they hunted him to teach him a lesson and keep their streets safe.

Actually, he always sneered at them with too much attitude and was unfriendly. Every time they walked by, he made really mean-spirited and bitchy comments about their clothes, often making them cry, he mocked their poverty. Once, he even cursed their mothers and called them "low budget welfare whores."

Or maybe he always paraded his homosexuality around the streets. Though this was America, he was still in Bushwick. He was asking for it, faggots need to be taught a lesson, fathers teach this, and religion says it is the right thing to do, he needed to be made a man.

No matter what, those boys were scared, he could have had a weapon, harmed them with a bag of rainbow-colored Skittles or something. All I know is he started it. He called them "spics!" If they didn't defend themselves, what would the law have done to protect our children?

25

ROUGH

Perhaps I am older but the pain remains the same.

Lube on the floor
causes slips down the stairs.
Broken condoms are possible statistics.

Sometimes marks simply appear.

Damaged body, damaged heart,
never forget—
bruises once brought pleasure to tricks,
counting cash
on your knees, swollen satisfying swollen.

Your uncle's favorite toy
mom's silent shame
you who should have died out on the street.

Still alive to experience this death.

EUCHARIST OF THE REFORMED WHORE

"This is my body, which is given up for you; do this in
remembrance of me."— 1Corinthians 11:24

i.

I'm afraid to finally meet him, unsure as to whether he will whisper
sweet nothings in that ear or already know and feel sorry for me. I

don't like to be viewed as a victim, uncomfortable talking about
that fateful night, always trying to hide the scar. I could say it was

from a motorcycle accident or bar brawl and come off
bad ass. It was nothing really. Before this, there was child abuse

and youth homelessness—another hustler on the streets trying to
survive in New York City. A disposable colored boy without a

future. With two good ears all I ever heard were the grunts of older
men, bad attempts at speaking Spanish, my own screams, police

sirens, the roar of approaching subways. Perhaps he has already
googled me and knows about my seedy past. It is a relief not to

have to tell him these stories. I don't remember what dating was
like before I started publishing my poems. Sex is sometimes

better with strangers. They do not try to be too gentle as if I
break easily. They do not get off abusing me the way they imagine

as a child my molester did. I wonder if he has also had a fucked
up life, found himself hungry or starving on purpose, attempted

suicide at least once, tried forgetting it all with drugs, allowed men to enter him without condoms, cried himself to sleep, tears heard

only with one good ear.

ii.

I didn't have freckles as a child.
They came about as I got older.
It seems I get a new one every time I hurt.

iii.

I'm a really bad judge of character. Before I started writing, I once
dated a handsome, muscular, Jewish guy and quickly befriended

his black roommate, Othniel. Cliff was the reason I stopped drug
dealing. They lived in a fabulous midtown penthouse. Cliff had

a great job and came from a wealthy family. I was living some
Pretty Woman fantasy. Cliff picked me up at a gay bar where I was

selling. One magical night together and I was his—making dinners,
redecorating his room, ironing clothes. Othniel was temperamental

with Cliff but always sweet and kind to me. You open up to
someone about your life, relate to them in so many ways, wonder if

you are dating the wrong person. Several years later, I had
published two poetry books and a novel. I was dating a police

officer who introduced me to a popular politician. My unlikely
transition from prostitute to poet inspired the Councilman so

much that he presented me with an award. It was a time that I felt
I had truly succeeded, turned my life around, survived. Othniel

followed my career. I ignored his phone calls and dinner
invitations. I had moved on and he was part of the life I left behind

with Cliff. You don't respond to messages from the past when they
attempt to haunt you. He was a reminder that I had made

mistakes, that things could have been different sooner. I didn't
know that he was now an aspiring politician, let alone friends with

the same Councilman. The news reporters sought me out, not

because my life had been worthy of film adaptation, as usual I was

about to be set up. My only mainstream news article mention was
when I dared to defend reappropriation, an oppressive word

—"spic." As an artist, I had no right as a Latino to take away its
power. Before this, it was when Othniel entered City Hall with a

gun, murdering the Councilman before killing himself too. I only
said nice things about him. I knew nobody else would.

Was I wrong to think there was a connection?

iv.

The guy in the back of the room asks me why it is essential that everything he reads about me mentions the fact I used to be a hustler. He doesn't get it.

"I've done a lot of work with queer homeless youth and it would be wrong to think that they are not hurt and angry and might possibly consider engaging in some sort of nefarious activity. Talking openly about my own mistakes in the past hopefully inspires them to understand that they have other options which perhaps I didn't or didn't know existed. If they can see how I have changed my life around, maybe they can see that there is hope for all of us to better ourselves."

I'm not sure I provided the answer he was looking for. I am fully aware that my back story is of great interest to others. It's hurt me

more than anything. I'm not really famous and I haven't won any prestigious literary awards. Perhaps I have sabotaged my own

flimsy career. But I am not ashamed. The only thing keeping me from the same despair that plagues most other poets is my sense

of humanity and humor. I haven't given up on myself even when others have. I never studied this craft in schools or had publicists

heralding me as the next best thing. Maybe someone should have been there to step in to keep me from damage control. I should

only consider writing poems that rhyme or are ideal for Hallmark cards. I could master metaphors or write about my toothbrush.

I'm considered an amateur. I've only made it this far because I am persistent. I have no swagger in the literary world—gay or Latino.

The only poet I could be compared to is Miguel Piñero. Or maybe Algarin. They don't care that I have always been explicit about my

sexuality or refused to be a junkie or alcoholic. My work is not so universal. That's alright with me. I won't make a living from this.

I'll get used to seeing my name misspelled. I'll remain disregarded. I'll die alone. End up back on the streets where I came from. The

ghosts of tranny hookers and boys gone too soon will come for me. After collecting my bones. We will disappear into the night.

Continue the party at the piers unnoticed as we always have. Dead to the world and forgotten. Never having shared our stories

because that would've been stereotypical. I know he thinks it is a crutch and I am being judged. In that moment it doesn't matter

that I have paid my dues in life.

v.

Maybe he will be scared of me. No matter how many times I get myself tested and come out negative I am always labeled 'tick-tick-boom.' I am a walking disease. I must keep a grid somewhere with the names of all the men I have been with—the ones with names I actually remember. Little boys are encouraged to seek sex and become men. But what happens when a man has already made a little girl out of you? It's that moment that defines everything you know and in between. How do you try to have a normal relationship when you were only normal for maybe three years in your entire life?

vi.

Men have enjoyed the softness of my skin.
Loved watching my face as they enter.
I am no longer a young boy or even a child.
Tell me ... is this how you like it?

I have had plentiful years of pleasuring older men.
Now I am the older one and still my role is the entertainment of
others. They want me to call them papi and devour whatever is left
that is exotic of me. More than my open mind, I have opened my

legs, my arms, my soul to multiculturalism. I have offered myself
as a piece in the name of peace. I have taken no prisoners in this
war waged by misguided love. I have tasted all the histories laid
out before me. Left my heart out on the streets while attempting

to refill its empty space. Strangers do not know how much it hurts
to feel anything more than their penetration. Maybe they need this
control over something, someone. They have been cheated on,
abandoned, frustrated with life. They rape my lands as I long to be

rediscovered. It has been this way since childhood. It is rare but
sometimes they want to settle into this new world. There is no
going back and they become one with this earth. Listening to my
stories as we stare out into the night sky—the stars shining within

us. Other times I fear being killed, dismembered, a cute freckled
face worn as a party mask or some lovely brown skin to hide under.
It's not only survivors of child abuse that often put themselves at risk.
We are all in danger of getting hurt emotionally or physically. It's

difficult to get into someone else's head when we can't get out of
our own. Unless, of course, it's been cut off and left in the fridge
with some really bad frostbite. Whether it is your soul or a part of
you, things always go missing in between love and war.

vii.

My ex-boyfriend—the cop—gets arrested for child abuse:

I finally understand why he broke up with me.

It now makes sense. The awkwardness of sex and meeting the
family so soon. The questions about being molested as a little
boy. Actually a baby. He would spend a lot of time with this
twelve-year-old boy, convincing all of us he was just trying to be
a really good big brother while I was left feeling neglected. I have
always looked younger than my age but, regardless of how much
I moisturize, I could never compete with a tween. Even when
I was hustling at the West Side Highway piers at sixteen, there
were twelve-year-old boys that I had to compete with. We were
underage but we were not looking to be saved by role models or
considered ourselves victims. We had already been damaged.
It's funny that I assumed he left me because I had a criminal
background and he was a respectable police officer and he's the
one that ended up behind bars. I cried for days because I had made
my sketchy past public and doomed myself from meeting someone
strong enough. Then I realized my darkness was something I left
behind, reinvented into art and, though I hurt myself, I never
hurt someone innocent. What I had felt was nothing compared to
what this boy must now live with. I know what he feels toward his
abuser. I know his life has been changed forever.

viii.

I eventually made peace with my cousin who sexually molested me as a child. I was visiting Ecuador in my early twenties and he had been deported there from the United States for drug dealing. He came to visit me with his girlfriend. He was dying of AIDS. I could have told him that, if there was a hell besides the life I had lived because of him, I truly hoped he ended up there—burning, rotting, experiencing twice the pain he caused me. He only saw that I was not destroyed. I did not tell him how easily I turned to prostitution and dealing, used drugs to numb the pain, kept men at a great distance or gave myself too freely, attempted suicide when I thought there was no hope. He stood there begging for forgiveness with his eyes, hoping to find compassion. Nothing needed to be said: I had survived; he was dead a few months later.

ix.

I have danced with murderers, child molesters, drug dealers,
prostitutes, probably serial killers, partied with them as they

fantasized victimizing my body. They have loved me the way a
father loves his child. They have seduced and left me wrestling

with my own darkness—unworthy of salvation. I found them
charming and thoughtful. Impressed to have been so desired

and wanted with all my spoils. I have shared my stories with them.
Cuddled in their arms comfortably waiting for the sun to rise.

Cocks hard as our naked bodies touch throughout the night.
Dreaming of what we could be for one another.

He—someone to take care and protect me from monsters.
Me—a handsome corpse.

I am still often awakened by someone entering me from behind.
I know how to keep quiet and take the pain. The driving force is

just companionship. I am simply blinded by my own demons and
desperation. It's hard to recognize disaster when you are too busy

trying to hide your own or avoiding it in the mirror. There is no
chance to settle for a common man. They want to cook for you,

play board games with their friends on weekends, require you to
sit through bad reality television and lousy movies. The only time

they dig deeper is when they are inside. They are afraid to love you
and are not strong enough to take you on as a challenge. Unlike

animals, they have no sense or instinct of true danger. I attract the ones crippled emotionally and capable of cutting me into pieces—

packing my torso into a worn suitcase dumped into a river. My heart would be removed, perhaps eaten with a dash of salt. He

would taste years of disappointment and tragedy. It would be tough to chew and too big to devour in just one meal. He would

need to seal it up tightly in a Ziploc bag and save some for later.

x.

He should know I
cannot cry out of
my right eye. It tends
to dry up. The other
one tears a lot. There
is no way he could
not notice.

xi.

December 2012

I am doing a reading with Amy Tan in San Francisco unaware
that my boyfriend in the audience is planning to break up with me

when we get back to New York just a week before Christmas. He's
in his forties and not out to his parents, even with an openly gay

brother and sister. It took him seven months to realize that I was
unapologetically gay. He calls us locas. He listens politely as I spew

my faggot shit from the mic. It gets better. That night he tells me
that his best friend in Chicago is a former gay who used to chase

after Asian trannies and is now married to a woman. I am even
more surprised than when he told me in a Boston hotel room that

he was planning to vote for Romney and also did not believe in
abortion. Not only did I lower my standards for someone with a

personal library made up of business books and fitness magazines
but I can't see I'm obviously dating a self-hating closet case. This is

the great fuckery of life. The gay activist dating the homophobe.
Either I write because I just can't make this shit up or shit follows

me because I'm likely to write about it.

xii.

I can be confusingly passionate with strangers in bed. I have no
problem giving freely of myself. It was once my profession. I have
been programmed since childhood to know how to make another
man feel desirable. I know how to smile and make it fun while
wondering when he'll leave. Sometimes I am really enjoying it.
Sometimes I'm just going through the motions. It's pretty hard
to tell the difference with me. Somewhere along the way I tricked
myself into thinking that I could be happy with someone I did not
love. I started believing my own lies. A memoir-like novel written
is just a part of the story. Perhaps even historical context. Secretly,
we all long to be challenged to reveal ourselves.

The trajectory of my love life so far
or, rather, the tragic story:

Young little boy unable to fully speak and a little feminine with
a tight hole. Tween in tight jeans unaware that he is gay. Naive
horny teen boy looking for true love meets crack addict. Underage
Latino boy hustling at the West Side Highway piers. Drugged up
club kid searching for a place to stay in the city for the night. Falls
in love with drug dealer and becomes one himself. The life of the
party selling favors in exchange for cash. Lost soul looking to be
saved by rich white man finds friendship with future murderer.
Young aspiring poet writes for even younger love interests before
falling in love and settling down with another recovering drug
addict. Broken-hearted thirty something meets police officer who
gets arrested for pedophilia. Author establishes long distance
relationship. Boyfriend decides not to move to New York. Ready
to throw in the towel, forty something man pursues sexless
relationship with thrift shop manager and then dates closeted
Republican. Appears never to have fully loved or been loved.

xiii.

I return to the West Side Highway piers. They are sanitized
and friendly. Welcoming. Children are now frequent visitors
as well as pets. Not us homeless House tweens and teens that
thought of ourselves as children and the animals society left us to
become back in the day. There are no longer haunting lampposts
illuminating the darkness of our souls. There is brightness and
hope and light. This place once stained with lube and cum is now a
great picnic spot. The grass is different. You cannot smoke it. The
Twin Towers that watched over us in the distance is now one single
parent. I could probably still turn a trick if I wanted but I am much
older and not desperate for a warm bed. It was here that Jose
& Luis vogued inside a parked jeep blaring "In The Mix" before
Madonna took them on tour. It was here Willi Ninja held court
and told me to write about us so that we would not all be forgotten.
It was here that I truly fell in love for the very first time with that
hustler named Supreme. The graffiti is gone and the air is now
full of reason. Though I preferred the decadence, I can still find a
certain peace here. And, yes, probably a 'piece' if I really wanted to.
I spent many nights living on this edge. The music faded. Friends
died. With only one good ear, I still hear the laughter. My dreams
are still the same. I fulfilled most of them except the one where I
fall in love and settle down. Turns out my time spent here affected
my entire life. I could have easily met any which one of the guys
I have dated throughout the years at this place. It is different
here now. I am different. The only thing we cannot change is our
history.

xiv.

He will maybe wonder what I am thinking about as he penetrates me. He will want to look into my eyes and feel my muscles relax around his stiffened cock. It will be his way of making sure that I am fully there in the moment. He will want to conquer me and treat me like a child. Perhaps he will stick his finger in my mouth to gently bite him and let him know the pain and pleasure I feel as he thrusts. He might even be the type to pin me down or choke me as he is pounding his way into me. Men want you to feel them and let them know that in that moment, at least, there is no other.

I have never known innocence.
I was born premature and out of wedlock.
I was three when I was sexually molested.
I was eleven when I messed around with another boy.
I was fifteen when I first made love.
I was sixteen when I began to sell my body.
I was nineteen when I got my first STD.
I was twenty-two when I passed out on drugs.
I was twenty-five when I started writing.
I was twenty-seven when I moved in with a lover.
I was thirty when I was divorced without marriage.
I was thirty-five when my life almost ended.
I was thirty-seven when I fell in love again.
I was thirty-nine when I was back on the market.
I have nothing left to offer but my heart.
In my forties, I don't have much anger left.
I'm sort of over it.

xvi.

I'm not quite sure I want to meet him. He lives in Austin and my life is in Brooklyn. Besides my long distance relationship with my ex in Albuquerque, I had a romance with a fellow writer in San Antonio. We would talk over the phone and write beautiful poems for one another. In the end, we were doomed. We were hurt boys, kindred spirits, comforting one another from the world outside. Our stories, etched in ink and scars, would exist beyond the night we spent together. San Antonio will always remind me of him. It would be hard to find a connection with anyone else there (other than sexually). I am tired of climbing mountains and long winding roads just to find my father. He is not any of the men that I meet out here on these streets or far away. He will not come to any of my readings or look for me on the internet. This guy I am being set up with won't be my savior. I will be misunderstood, a freak. He will take my inappropriate jokes the wrong way and leave me the same way I arrived—full of hope and insecure.

xvii.

I'm not quite sure how many men I have been with.
I don't know how many times I have fallen in love.
I never kept count of all my tricks and hook-up's.
I have no idea how many times I could've been killed.
I suppose I have died many times over.
Yet, I'm alive and breathing.
I'm capable of finding what I never had.
I've lost so many friends along this journey.
It's a fucking miracle that I'm still here.

xviii.

Nothing has changed.
I like to look into their eyes
to catch a glimpse of him.
Any of them could be my father.

xix.

I will die alone in my bed. My cat Alexis will eat me. He will chew away at the flesh that comforted so many men. The blood that miraculously survived the threat that plagued others will supply him with nourishment. Better him to enjoy this body than some

cannibal. I will have never met him. The idea of him will be gone forever along with the memory of me. People will say that I wasted my entire life looking to find him. He might get word of my passing and wonder what it would have been like to have known me.

Through stories I have written and photographs, he might imagine the world I left behind. I had a tragic life that could have been very different if he had been part of it. Poems would have brought smiles and my soul would have found its gateway to the other side.

But I know my ghost will simply linger. It will remain in search of him. Men will feel my presence moving through them hoping to be touched. In life, many hands lay upon me but none ever felt my spirit. It had been lost since the age of three.

xx.

My best friend is getting married to his boyfriend of five years during the summer. I tell my mother and she surprisingly wants to attend the wedding. We've had a tumultuous journey together but we've come a long way. She has no idea how hard it has been for me to find true love. I know she wants me to find peace and be happy now. It's in her excitement for them.

I'm inspired again to remain open to the possibility of settling down. I know she wants this for me. She wants to have a son-in-law and perhaps grandchildren. The woman that put me out at sixteen for being gay wants the man that survived to feel loved. We have both failed but there is still a chance for me. I've just been giving myself away to all the wrong men.

xxi.

April 6, 2013

Outside, the weather is getting warmer as spring finally struggles
to arrive. It has been cold for much too long. I can feel the warmth
of the sun. Alexis is sleeping peacefully in my bed. My mother
called to remind me to ask my best friend to invite her to the
wedding with his partner. I am leaving in a few weeks to celebrate
Fiesta with my friend and meet this guy in San Antonio. I have
not heard from him. No text. No voice message. No Facebook.
I have written a letter of support to a judge for my pedophile
former police officer ex who will soon be getting out of prison. I
have dusted off the City Council Citation that I received from the
gunned down politician who I now see in subway ads as having
donating his eyes after death. I have also checked in with my
recovered drug addict ex who is now positive and lives in Florida.
I have no plants or flowers in my apartment to cater to. I'm still
in one piece and no one dug deep and pulled my heart out to eat
it. I have lotioned my skin but no one has taken it to be the life
of the party. It's okay if I never hear from him or even meet him.
I'm almost forty-three and I've been used to this since the age of
three. For decades ... four decades ... I've learned to be alone. It's
a suitable life. I've been obsessed with love and death. There's
still hope for one and the other will inevitably come for me soon
enough. I just hope for a beautiful day and that I am aware when it
is time for me to go and never look back.

MEMORABLE

Yes, there was a blizzard starting outside—the streets filled with panicked pedestrians trying to make their way home. But you kissed me as I had hoped for, sweet and inspired, after great conversation and coffee. There was no trace of alcohol on your breath and we didn't head back to a tent or apartment. This spontaneous first date featured winds picking up around us and icy snow pelting against our embrace. Neither of us would let this moment pass (news reports called for inclement weather) though we both knew this storm would soon.

REDUNDANT

I have no clue how our story will begin.
The rooftop at The Eagle was not particularly crowded
for a Friday night.
Shirtless daddies, muscle bears, leather queens—
we didn't exactly fit yet we belonged.
Why were we even there? Doesn't really matter.
You bought me a Stoli and tonic—my favorite.
This was before the boycott of Russian vodka
but I never identified being gay with alcohol.
You would drive me to the train station afterward but before this,
I touched your nipple ring and we kissed.
I could tell, between us, we've tasted any number of lips—
sometimes truly special, mostly mechanical.
Both probably wondering if we would end up sleeping together and
 if it would be wise.
It's just been done so many times.
Honestly, I'd rather go home and cuddle with my cat
which you seem to be allergic to.
It's okay for us to embrace being alone and not feel lonely.
But I live in this skin that has only ever wanted that special touch.
Ironic that this moment brought life to a dead soul I suppose.
Be mine forever or move on to someone else.
Walking home later, I text you about a great time
knowing you are leaving for Spain for a few weeks—
it's my luck. I have no control over these things
and, still, I make myself a fool by trying too hard.
Hopeless. Helpless. Hapless.
After all, this novel was over before it even began.
Another one about heartbreak. Another one about hurt.
Love. Again with love. I've since been kissed by another guy
(and it meant nothing at all except perhaps entertaining friends
out on the town for a bachelor party as somebody needed to be the

slut). Learn to love yourself.

Love. A best friend's wedding. I enjoy my bed with an open window and a cool breeze.

Spread. Comfortable. Books on the side. We are all words: meaningful. I wake up mornings feeling complete.

Have a routine with too much ambition.

A sentence without proper punctuation.

DEAD

I thought he loved me
because of the way he pointed out the stars
in the night sky and knew the constellations
The word was never in our vocabulary
Holding each other tightly in bed—
the closest expression shared of mutual want and desire
I felt ashamed amongst my friends
I, the one who once upon a time was a paid professional
in the art of sex
I, the one who had fulfilled so many fantasies
Left behind, untouched
Perhaps he thought of my dying with him
until realizing, only this lesbian bed death provided silence
from my life
filled with dreams and laughter
as he forced himself to smile in public, in private
He said, "We will definitely be friends. I promise!"
And I never saw him again
I'm not quite sure I ever really did

THE WAY WE ARE
(OR PERHAPS JUST THE WAY THAT I AM)

There are no lullabies
for damaged children
used as sex slaves right out of cribs
Never a chance
to be wholesome

Self-destructively standing
on the edge of rooftops
to be swallowed up by the world below
No religion
available to heal our souls

You watch us lusting
drunk off intercourse
desiring affection from strangers
revisiting torment

We give ourselves freely
disappoint when we don't
because we want what others can have—
to be more than broken toys

Our hearts—
love stories written with pencils
for simple erasure
until the next one comes along

We are house trained animals
fodder for human friendship
until they settle and we are boring
tragic in our needs
fading unnoticed into the background

We are demons disguised as poets
falsely expressing concern for politics and social justice
infiltrating the respectable ranks of true artists

We are threatening in our free-spiritedness
comfortable in unknown beds
willing to fulfill fantasies
easily and too readily

We are temptation
darkness and decadence
covered by thick skin
daring and desirable
toned from all the running (away)
promising the casualness of laughter
sweet goodbyes in the morning
smiles on the subway ride home
and damned if we want anything more

We survive independently
express creatively
rock stars with devoted fans
loving the audacity we learned much too young

We are filled with loneliness
praying for someone to love us
to find that lost innocence
wanting our fathers
to save us
from monsters

HATS OFF TO THE BULL

I failed to see the signs along the way
confused by my needs
only to be told not to overthink,
overfeel, overwant, overdesire.

I didn't recognize the misery
I laughed with. The regret in your eyes
settled into your features, stories of
dead fathers, heartbreak, tears.

You did me no favors by holding back,
remaining distant as I longed for you,
sleeping alone with you right by my side,
contemplating your escape.

You once gave me a clock, aware
our time was running out. Your soul
belonged to the ghost haunting your life,
an empty house, full of could-have-beens.

Capable of change, I tried for us.
Not because you asked, because I was ready.
You have your freedom back. Now, lose yourself.
Just remember I was once a man

worth kissing. Goodbye. Hats off to the bull.
Believe in yourself and forget my sorrow.
Someday, I might smile at you again
and the red flags I will no longer ignore.

TRESPASS

Were't not that you were repulsive on your underside or on any side, whatever humanity left within me might take pity on your hideous corpse. Did he have mercy and kill you instantaneously or were you a momentary play thing after incapacitation? The beast is sovereign ruler of this household. The uninvited are subject to torture. In life, you likely ran really fast and could maybe even fly (jealous!). You were a scavenger but he is a hunter by nature, bored waiting for my arrival each day. Perhaps it was the starch in my bookbindings or my manuscripts that was cause for the break in. I didn't train him to be a ninja. I don't care to decapitate you and keep your head in my fridge. I will hide your filthy, tiny body in my version of some mini-suitcase and toss you into the nearest river (my toilet). Tonight, we celebrate with treats!

LOS HIJOS DE MAGDALENA

Hay tantos muertos que fingen vivir entre nosotros
que pertenecen a una iglesia oculta tras la cosecha de odio
que nos toma y nos parpadea fuera con ojos ignorantes
y nos condena por acostarnos
juntos en las tumbas de nuestras camas
mientras su salvador cuelga de clavos, en vitrina de paredes huecas
y nuestros sacrificios los dejamos colgados en cercas
sangrando ríos de gloria para quitar los pecados de su mundo

Este prejuicio es el dolor que nubla mis ojos y anuda mi espina
las cicatrices detrás de mi cabeza
grabadas por los que ofrecen brazos abiertos
sangrando de hipocresía, sueños perdidos, y mantras intangibles
aquellos que atormentan nuestras oraciones diarias
con los sonidos de opresión
para silenciar nuestros pastores con muerte
porque la muerte iguala sueños que nunca serán escuchados
y nuestros profetas no logran encontrar mapas hacia la salvación

Pero el viento no heredará los ecos de nuestras almas
no dejaremos nuestros lienzos con colores, pero sin acabar
ni quedaremos niños sin invitación de un Dios menor
moleremos nuestros pies descubiertos con los dedos en la tierra
escucharemos las campanillas en la locura de la vida
prenderemos velas para nuestros hermanos y hermanas
desde la isla de Puerto Rico
a las muelles de Nueva York
a las granjas de Laramie, Wyoming
a las calles de Castro, San Francisco
y nos sentiremos lo más cercano posible al cielo
porque el amor verdadero no tiene fronteras
y nuestros ángeles también tienen alas

THE REASON

Because you tried to kiss me on the first date
in the front row of a crowded theater
before the movie started,
after snorting cocaine in the bathroom;
because of those arrogant eyes,
glazed by self-destructive frustration;
because of those futile lips
forcing against my face
assuming a crucifix or winning lottery ticket;
because of that smirk, revealing egotistical conquest
like another prey, a kingdom to possess
as if the gods had sanctioned your spell:

The residue in your nostrils damaged your view
with misguided judgment,
my love is a tree existing alone on a mountain
less like a forest
and definitely not one for you to smoke.

MARRIAGE & BONUS REWARD POINTS

March 26, 2013—The Supreme Court seems weary on a broad gay marriage ruling. I've already accepted at this stage of my life and after many failed relationships that the only aisle I will ever be walking down is perhaps the vitamin section at the local pharmacy.

I could wear all white but the cashier would probably just think I practiced Santeria. *Dead chicken in aisle six!* I am meeting someone in a few weeks that a friend is setting me up with but I haven't even heard from him lately. It makes it hard to imagine

what our lives would be like and if I should pick him up some mouthwash or deodorant. I don't understand why we are struggling for the same rights everyone else has. Religion has absolutely nothing to do with whether two people are truly in

love or not. If I'm holding hands with another guy down the River Walk and some kid asks their parents about same sex relationships, that's for them to explain as a family. I've been abused, abandoned, self-destructive and victimized for too long to

back down for homophobia. The only real fear they have is that we are just like them—capable of either enduring love or dramatic divorces. Marriage is not even about procreation. I could totally skip the pregnancy test aisle already crowded by fabulous

independent women. If it doesn't happen this time around, it will very soon. The revolution will not be brought to you by Wal-Mart but it will most certainly require a shopping cart.

June 26, 2013—The Supreme Court strikes down the Defense of Marriage Act and dismisses Prop 8. Same-sex marriage becomes a federal right. I wear white and head to the local pharmacy to soak up the blood on aisle six.

FORSAKEN

*"Perhaps when we find ourselves wanting everything, it is
because we are dangerously close to wanting nothing"*
—Sylvia Plath

I found out about my ex-boyfriend Michael's nephew last night—
how he had shot himself in the face at fourteen. I only remembered
him as a beautiful baby and never imagined that bullying would
inspire him to pull a trigger on himself. His parents were fuckin'
awesome and it really hurt to think about this painful reality. If I
believed in God, I would have prayed for his soul. This would have
been the same God that allowed my innocence to be taken away
at age three. It is hard to believe in something that has never been
there for you. I suppose my ex felt the same. In a matter of a few
short years, he lost his father, brother, mother, sister and now
nephew. We had had a tumultuous break up but even I did not
harbor such cruel feelings for him or anybody for that matter. Not
like this God. It was just a few months ago that his sister Laura
had been displaced by Hurricane Sandy out in Staten Island. I
loved Laura and it was hard to grasp the idea that she had lost
everything. She was allowed by FEMA to go back for just one
weekend to gather whatever she could from her destroyed home.
Laura was found dead the next morning in her bed. Struggling
with weight and health issues and now losing everything to a really
bad storm—her heart gave out. There were rumors of potential
drug use but I chose to remember her as a devoted mother. I
did not attend the funeral. Her daughter Ashley reached out to
me on Facebook shortly after. Now in her early twenties, she
remembered me from when she was five, the little girl we took to
see a Barbie Dream House at Toys-R-Us, Times Square. I still have
many pictures with her and my kittens (and her Barbie dolls, of
course!) I would love babysitting her with Michael and dressing
her up in drag. She knew nothing of how her uncle disappeared

for days on drug binges and woke up in someone else's arms. After I found out he had cheated on me with a childhood friend, we agreed to stay together but would invite other men to join us for sex. I suppose he convinced me it was only fair. But that motherfucker got off watching other men have sex with me. He eventually started doing cocaine again and it was when I pushed his druggie ass that—with just one punch—he knocked me to the ground. I got a black eye and lost some teeth and we finally broke up. I went to work the next day and claimed to have fallen down a flight of stairs. Very Sable Colby from that *Dynasty* spin-off. Years later, when I was brutally attacked by a group of teens on the streets of Brooklyn, I also went to work the next day and probably claimed the same fall. I was clumsy but you still had to pay the rent and the cable bill. I suppose I was trained for this as a child. Every time my mother beat me for getting out of line or being just a little too gay, I would go to school claiming all kinds of accidents. I remember once I ended up in the hospital with a bloody wound to the back of my head. Before getting stitched, the doctors and nurses kept asking how this happened, and, with my mother in the room, I remained silent. It's funny that I was never one for violence but it always seemed to make its way into my life. I have the scars to prove it. Nonetheless, anyone who has been with me in bed can attest to how affectionate I tend to be. Perhaps because it was seriously lacking in my life as a child or maybe it's my daddy issues but I love cuddling with someone I'm really into. I don't even have to love them or hardly know them. Endearing myself to naked strangers is my forte. This is why I was such a great hustler during my formative teen years. I think the happy endings were more for me than for my customers (and I got paid for doing what I enjoyed). There has never been God in my life except for men I turned to as father figures. I have cried so much throughout life but when I watch something on television or read a good book, it all goes away. This is why I love entertainment. But then you go back to dating and find out you are nothing more than damaged goods. The psychoanalyst you had a great date with Googles you and decides you're probably better suited to be his patient than a partner. The guy you dated for months, who is in his forties and is still not out to his parents, decides you are too *loca* for him and there is no future for the two of you. Even though he has an openly gay brother and sister. Most of your close friends are dead from AIDS or about to get married and there is no one to turn to. Your wingmen have moved on to the afterlife or the altar and you find yourself an aging rock star. I won't say I am famous because nobody really knows me. I mean, really. I hate it when a date asks what it feels like to be well known, rather unknown. I should realize right there and then that it is all kinds of doomed. But I'm still here. I haven't offed myself or gotten killed. Maybe someday someone will read about Michael or his nephew or Laura and wonder, like me, if there really is a God. People die everyday and children are bullied at school all the time. You could take an elevator with somebody and know nothing about them—how they lived or how they are slowly dying. Maybe they will smile and it will brighten up your world, unaware of how much that small gesture of humanity really means.

THE HUSTLER

He sizes me up and caresses
his muscular chest before grabbing
his hardening bulge. He is all
masculinity and sex, the
contempt in his eyes hidden
within the shadows underneath
his baseball cap. Was I ever this
aggressive? I remember being
coy and flirtatious, but then, my
aesthetic was youth and lost
innocence. I know his hunger
and the fun knowing what his
body is capable of and the hot
fluids that produce dead
presidents. He wants to devour
me with the hopes I could be his
savior for the night. I want to
dare to make out with him, offer
myself passionately, hoping that
he will take advantage of my
need, take what he wants and
leave, that he will understand I
was once him, counting the
money before fading. He will
think himself successful as I
once did. I want to offer him
advice, the kind I never got, the
kind that could have changed my
life. I know it to be meaningless,
to be lost as soon as the cock
rises, as soon as you are fed and
you make it to another day. He

will disappear unaware he just
hustled with his future.

NAKED

They fucked up your tattoo!
That man on the crucifix is supposed to be completely nude
Balls hanging
Where did that loincloth come from?
Your tattoo artist could sketch fabric on to your skin
but not a cock?
Obviously he or she was not a Roman
because they offered no such kind gestures to criminals
Didn't they read that sacred book?
It doesn't mention anything about covering his private parts
How could they modify your Savior?
At least he's got those true-to-life details—
long blonde hair, blue eyes and ivory white skin

SAVIOR

for Piri Thomas

My vulnerability in front of an audience,
it provides connection. Electrical charge.
Approachable touch. Welcome embrace.
Deceit in fruition.

I stand upon this stage
a narcissistic prophet. Illuminating lights
providing halo effects.
Your Christ on a cross
until declaring myself gay.

There is no need to excuse
yourself from judgment.
I have learned to live within this box.
Yield assumptions of weakness with sassy comments.
Speak. A factory line homosexual creation
for American consumption.
Of course, I love Madonna and Broadways musicals.
Of course, I can fake the lisp of stereotypes.

But I am also more than Puerto Rican
heat and Ecuadorian mountains
baptized in Santero myths;
the causes you expect me to fight for;
expressing the tragedies of others, their struggles.
My heart is a casket
carrying the dead body of my boyhood soul
and the solitude of words never uttered.

My eyes are as dark as the rooms

in which children are abused.
Bright as the power of revelation.
Alive as the night sky.
I read from pages; avoid contact.
Girls and boys like us learn not to stare.

Live in my skin
if this fever is not too much to bear—
full of desire and passion.
The awkwardness of non-virgin children
reflecting abused adults in the mirror.

Our trust is a cold windy road
with no one around to guide us home,
lurking in shadows
much like animals you know are
there but cannot see.

I am capable of finding happiness.
Refusing to become all those
things I was left behind to be.
I am possible to love
because I have been hurt.
Safely emerging from so many hands.
secret hiding places intact.
Remembering only laughter.
Learning to talk to express pain
and pleasure and peace.

Silence cannot start conversations.
Poems are museums containing art.
They must be shared with others,
written by candlelight but read loudly,
holding nothing back.
Perhaps even saying too much
but never enough.

Yeah, I have warmed many beds.
Given freely of myself.
Joked to my own disadvantage
but my rest belongs to me.
I will sleep comfortably only with
the right one—not dictator, or tyrant,
or hypocrite—he who shares these dreams.

I am born anew at each A.M.
In the arms of my father figure.
Down these mean streets
I too have learned to survive.

UNBLOSSOMED

The grey skies outside, the ominous clouds, the chill in the air
futile threats against the warmth of your heart,
the splendor of your smile
This storm will pass washing away sorrow
hope blossoming with your touch

Chase away these demons
Allow me to unfurl within your arms
Heal these bruises purple from war . . .

i.

Those were the words I had originally started writing
I was about to share them with him
the night he announced there was no future for us
This was a week before Christmas
and a week after our trip to San Francisco
According to Mayan predictions,
the world was set to end a few days later but mine
had already fallen apart
Nothing terribly exciting happened on 12/21/12—
my cat still longed for me

ii.

I put my life at risk
convinced this would be forever and yet he said
there was 'no spark' between us
I suppose out of insecurity,
I was committed to making this work—they say
sacrifice is everything
In more than just Biblical terms, I have literally been a whore

Besides emotional baggage, I am physically handicapped—
deaf in my right ear
The advantages are an open-mind and only one ear plug
to drown out snoring
Friends have died and children have been killed
My tears—this poem—inspired by yet another failed relationship

iii.

Thanks to my father,
I've been used to being abandoned by men since I was born
Between my mother and stepfather, I had such
a fucked up childhood,
it's a good thing I didn't march myself up to an orphanage
and put myself up for adoption
but, strangely enough, this never stopped me
from believing in true love—
unattainable as it has seemingly been for me

iv.

I don't know what I dreamed of before being molested as a child—
perhaps the comfort of wild beasts
I knew of innocence once, even if only for a handful of years
There is no love for tainted children or a forgiving God or heaven
We only provide temporary pleasure
before undamaged pastures are sought
I have given myself freely
if only to rest inside an embrace and believe
in the possibility of being wanted
I hope to lift the weight of this heavy heart,
dropping it to watch it burst as it hits the hell below—
the only world I have ever known

v.

I no longer have my youth and my strength has stumbled
It has been years since I turned to drugs or drinks for comfort
Hopeless romantics at this age are simply hopeless
This soul is nothing more than a lesson to be learned,
a pool for reflection
for those fortunate enough not to have had gritty pasts

vi.

Years spent trying to pass as a wallflower unseen
leads some to the stage to blossom
Silence is not encouraged; revelations are applauded
No one cares what happens when you exit
or those you have distanced
It's all about winning the game before spreading your wings
to fade into sunlight

vii.

Outside—the chill in the air, the ominous clouds, the grey skies
Your heart—futile threat against the warmth and splendor
of my smile
Your sorrow—a storm that will not pass
Your touch—unblossomed

I chase away my own demons
Allow myself to unfurl in the arms of others
Bruises purple from war heal

WHY IT TOOK SO LONG

It took years for us to finally settle down
because the full blue moon only comes around every so often
hurricanes and tropical storms needed to pass
we needed more pedophile priests at the Vatican and a new Pope
and cicadas needed to prepare for their swarm
because we had to be more broken
regardless of how much we already suffered
anticipating death and all its promises
with only hope to keep us going

It took years because we needed to catch up to one another

It took years like the woman who kicked me out for being gay
to eventually attend gay weddings protected by federal law
thanks to a black president or finally getting a job in publishing
and making my way to cities I had not yet visited
because we had to accept lone wolves are sometimes lonely
late at night
and casual sex with different types of men
is fun but there is always fear and lingering doubt
because pets and pillows do not cuddle back as necessary
and we had the right to be messy
It took years
because we needed to find ourselves
before these ancient souls could one another

I have no other theory, besides maybe kismet,
why it took so many years

I was not ready to fall for your smile
or allow myself the joy of hearing your voice
I could not taste your lips in return

hungering for that perfect heavenly kiss
where nothing and no one around us matters
and I am unafraid of getting beat down again
or being left completely deaf this time
It took years
because it would have been a mistake then
at that period in our lives, before gentrification
and if we hadn't found our way back to each other
we'd be lost spirits searching for that door
I am not pretending to be spiritual by any means,
but I am grateful we finally walked through it

Whitney found out what she'd been missing
always on the run
the fact that I found you and never my own father
makes me realize I was never even looking for him after all
his touch would have creeped me out
instead of providing your comfort
It took years
because we were sleepless but not living in Seattle
and sometimes the snow comes down in June like Vanessa says
so we just had to wait for global warming
to substantially change our weather
It took years because I can't fall asleep with the television on
and I am a morning person in spite of my denial
because we needed to develop some greys in our hair
and realize aging is beautiful when there is love involved
because the God you pray to in all His or Her wisdom
thought it would be funny to make us wait for it
and made the time pass
because there was little hope that later in life
the years would bring us together

It took years
because maybe it was meant to be
that we needed to struggle for this

more than surviving poverty, addiction and disease
It took years because we needed to change
to appreciate love
because we both ended up at that bar one Saturday
night and knew that it was the right time for us
to look forward to many more years,
this time, together

STEP FATHER

He forgets that he used to call me *mariconcito*—
that I harbored years of hatred toward him
while hoping to find my real father. My
childhood memories of him reminding me
I was my mother's son, not his. I tried
to poison him once and scattered sharp nails
inside the shoes in his closet. By the time one
of his sons died of AIDS I was already lost
in contempt for the man I blamed for everything.
There was the time I was in love and he met my
boyfriend. Now he forgets to go to the bathroom

or where he is but he still remembers Michael
and asks about him. I help him walk slowly
outdoors to step outside the prison cell that is
the tiny apartment with no windows in which
I grew up abused by both of them. He barely
understands. His fate has been torture. I know
that I cannot be his savior. I used to pray for
him to die but here he is slowly fading. In his
eyes I see that he learned to love me and wishes
he could take it all back. He is unable to recall
those drunken nights and hateful words. I should

do the same. I left a long time ago but he still
remains haunted by the little boy who wanted
to belong. Like him, I want to forget that we
made mistakes and caused so much pain. I need
for both of us to remember how he taught me
how to ride a bike and how to swim and told
me, better late than never, that he loved me and
was proud of all I had done. I have to help him

settle into his favorite chair and let him know that I forgive him. There is a place somewhere where he will call me *hijo* and I will know him as my dad.

Special Thanks to Sven Davisson, Shelly Weiss, Wendy Jenkins, Carlos Acevedo, Avina Ichele Ross, Eric Thomas Norris, Robert Siek, Jennie Livingston, Christopher Bram, Trebor Healey, Lesléa Newman, Stephen S. Mills, Eduardo C. Corral, Felice Picano, Rigoberto Gonzalez, Meryl Meisler, Sophia Wallace, Leonardo Toro, Rodney Allen Trice, Stephanie Holley, Lorenzo Herrera y Lozano, Dino Foxx, David Caleb Acevedo, Charlie Vazquez, Charles Rice-Gonzalez, my friends and colleagues at Penguin Random House and The LGBT Network, my lovely parents and Alexis Dylan Xavier

For more information on Emanuel Xavier
visit www.emanuelxavier.com

CPSIA information can be obtained at www.ICGtesting.com
Printed in the USA
BVOW02s1649201013

334135BV00002B/5/P